The Wisdom of Jesus
Parables that Transform Lives

By Albert Barzaga

Introduction

Welcome to a profound and transformative journey through the parables of Jesus, where wisdom and grace intertwine to offer you a refreshing perspective on life and divine love. This book will not only take you through ancient stories but will invite you to discover how these timeless teachings can illuminate your path today.

Each parable is a window into Jesus' deep understanding of human nature and God's unconditional love. These stories, told with both simplicity and depth, aim not to impose rules or judgments but to invite you into a personal experience of grace and freedom. Within them, you will find not only spiritual principles but also guidance and answers for everyday challenges.

As you delve into these pages, I encourage you to open your heart and mind. Allow Jesus' wisdom to speak directly to your being, revealing liberating truths and a love that surpasses all understanding. There is no need to follow a rigid path to enjoy these teachings; rather, it is the sincere desire to understand and grow that will lead you to a rich and transformative experience.

Discover the power of the parables and let their lessons resonate in your life, guiding you towards greater peace, love, and understanding. This is a journey of grace and revelation, and you are invited to be a part of it. Welcome, and may you enjoy this exploration of divine wisdom.

Table of Contents

13. The Parable of the Talents

- Introduction
- Context and Meaning
- Lessons of Responsibility and Purpose
- Reflections and Applications

14. The Parable of the Two Sons

- Introduction
- Context and Meaning
- Lessons of Obedience and Repentance
- Reflections and Applications

15. The Wicked Tenants

- Introduction
- Context and Meaning
- Lessons of Divine Justice and Grace
- Reflections and Applications

Chapter 1: The Good Samaritan

Introduction

The parable of the Good Samaritan is one of the most cherished and well-known stories Jesus told. It can be found in the Gospel of Luke, chapter 10, verses 25-37. This parable invites us to reflect on the true meaning of loving our neighbor and challenges us to live according to divine grace and compassion.

Jesus told this story in response to a question from an expert in the law who wanted to know who his neighbor was. In His answer, Jesus offers a lesson in wisdom that transcends cultural and religious boundaries, showing that true love has no limits.

Here is the full citation of the parable:

Luke 10:25-37 (NLT):

25. One day an expert in religious law stood up to test Jesus by asking him this question: "Teacher, what should I do to inherit eternal life?" 26. Jesus replied, "What does the law of Moses say? How do you read it?"

27. The man answered, "'You must love the lord your God with all your heart, all your soul, all your strength, and all your mind.' And, 'Love your neighbor as yourself.'"

28. "Right!" Jesus told him. "Do this and you will live!"

29. The man wanted to justify his actions, so he asked Jesus, "And who is my neighbor?"

30. Jesus replied with a story: "A Jewish man was traveling from Jerusalem down to Jericho, and he was attacked by bandits. They stripped him of his clothes, beat him up, and left him half dead beside the road.

31. "By chance a priest came along. But when he saw the man lying there, he crossed to the other side of the road and passed him by.

32. A Temple assistant walked over and looked at him lying there, but he also passed by on the other side.

33. "Then a despised Samaritan came along, and when he saw the man, he felt compassion for him.

34. Going over to him, the Samaritan soothed his wounds with olive oil and wine and bandaged them. Then he put the man on his own donkey and took him to an inn, where he took care of him.
35. The next day he handed the innkeeper two silver coins, telling him, 'Take care of this man. If his bill runs higher than this, I'll pay you the next time I'm here.'

36. "Now which of these three would you say was a neighbor to the man who was attacked by bandits?" Jesus asked.

37. The man replied, "The one who showed him mercy."Then Jesus said, "Yes, now go and do the same."

Context and Meaning

To better understand this parable, it's important to know the context in which Jesus told it. At that time, Samaritans and Jews did not get along; there was deep animosity between them. Jesus used this cultural tension to illustrate a crucial point about love and mercy.

In the parable, a man is attacked by robbers while traveling from Jerusalem to Jericho. He is left half-dead on the roadside. First, a priest passes by, and then a Levite, but both ignore the man and continue on their way. Finally, a Samaritan—someone who was despised by the Jews—stops to help the injured man. He tends to his wounds, takes him to an inn, and ensures he receives care until he recovers.
The message of Jesus is clear: our neighbor is not defined by race, religion, or nationality, but by our ability to show compassion and love. True divine wisdom is manifested in acts of mercy and kindness to all, without distinction.

Lessons of Grace and Compassion

The parable of the Good Samaritan teaches us several key lessons about grace and compassion:

1. **Boundless Love:** Jesus shows us that true love transcends barriers and prejudices. The Samaritan, considered an enemy by the Jews, is the hero of the story because he showed mercy and compassion.

2. **Practical Action:** Love is not just a feeling but an action. The Samaritan did not just feel compassion; he acted to relieve the suffering of the injured man. This challenges us to put our faith into practice through concrete acts of kindness.

3. **Personal Initiative:** The Samaritan took the initiative to help, without expecting anything in return. This willingness to act, even when it is inconvenient or when others choose to ignore the need, is a powerful example of how divine wisdom operates in our lives.

Reflections and Applications

To apply the wisdom of this parable in our daily lives, we can reflect on the following questions:

1. **Who do we consider our neighbor?** The parable challenges us to expand our definition of neighbor to include all people, especially those who are different from us.

2. **How can we show love and compassion in our daily actions?** Identify specific ways in which you can help those in need, whether through small or large acts.

3. **Are we willing to take the initiative to help others, even when it is inconvenient?** The Samaritan's willingness to help, despite the difficulties, is a powerful example of how we should live our faith.

Remember that the divine wisdom Jesus taught through this parable centers on love and compassion. By following these principles, we can

live in accordance with God's grace and make a meaningful difference
in the world around us.

Chapter 2: The Prodigal Son

Introduction

The Parable of the Prodigal Son is a deeply moving story told by Jesus,
found in the Gospel of Luke, chapter 15, verses 11-32. This parable
reveals profound truths about unconditional love and forgiveness,
showcasing the boundless grace of God. It illustrates the nature of
true repentance and the joy of reconciliation.

Jesus shared this parable to emphasize the depth of God's love for
every individual, no matter how far they have strayed. It speaks to the
heart of anyone who has ever felt lost or unworthy, offering a
message of hope and redemption.

Context and Meaning

To grasp the full meaning of the Parable of the Prodigal Son, it is
essential to understand the context in which Jesus told it. The story
was addressed to the Pharisees and scribes, who were grumbling
about Jesus' association with sinners and tax collectors. By telling this
parable, Jesus aimed to reveal the nature of God's grace and the joy
that comes from repentance and forgiveness.

In the parable, a younger son demands his share of the inheritance
and leaves home, squandering his wealth in reckless living. When a

famine arises, he finds himself in dire need and decides to return to his father, acknowledging his mistakes. The father, filled with compassion, welcomes him back with open arms and celebrates his return. The elder brother, who stayed and worked dutifully, becomes resentful of the celebration for his wayward brother.

The father's response to the elder son's complaint reveals the central message of the parable: the joy of forgiveness and the importance of celebrating every return to grace.

Here is the full citation of the parable:

Luke 15:11-32 (NLT):

11. To illustrate the point further, Jesus told them this story: "A man had two sons.

12. The younger son told his father, 'I want my share of your estate now before you die.' So his father agreed to divide his wealth between his sons.

13. "A few days later this younger son packed all his belongings and moved to a distant land, and there he wasted all his money in wild living.

14. About the time his money ran out, a great famine swept over the land, and he began to starve.

15. He persuaded a local farmer to hire him, and the man sent him into his fields to feed the pigs.

16. The young man became so hungry that even the pods he was feeding the pigs looked good to him. But no one gave him anything.

17. "When he finally came to his senses, he said to himself, 'At home even the hired servants have food enough to spare, and here I am dying of hunger!

18. I will go home to my father and say, "Father, I have sinned against both heaven and you,

19. and I am no longer worthy of being called your son. Please take me on as a hired servant."'

20. "So he returned home to his father. And while he was still a long way off, his father saw him coming. Filled with love and compassion, he ran to his son, embraced him, and kissed him.

21. His son said to him, 'Father, I have sinned against both heaven and you, and I am no longer worthy of being called your son.'

22. "But his father said to the servants, 'Quick! Bring the finest robe in the house and put it on him. Get a ring for his finger and sandals for his feet.

23. And kill the calf we have been fattening. We must celebrate with a feast,

24. for this son of mine was dead and has now returned to life. He was lost, but now he is found.' So the party began.

25. "Meanwhile, the older son was in the fields working. When he returned home, he heard music and dancing in the house,

26. and he asked one of the servants what was going on.

27. 'Your brother is back,' he was told, 'and your father has killed the fattened calf. We are celebrating because of his safe return.'

28. "The older brother was angry and wouldn't go in. His father came out and begged him,

29. but he replied, 'All these years I've slaved for you and never once refused to do a single thing you told me to. And in all that time you never gave me even one young goat for a feast with my friends.

30. Yet when this son of yours comes back after squandering your money on prostitutes, you celebrate by killing the fattened calf!'

31. "His father said to him, 'Look, dear son, you have always stayed by me, and everything I have is yours.

32. We had to celebrate this happy day. For your brother was dead and has come back to life! He was lost, but now he is found!'"

Lessons of Unconditional Love and Forgiveness

The Parable of the Prodigal Son teaches us several vital lessons about unconditional love and forgiveness:
1. **Unconditional Love:** The father's reaction to his son's return reflects the nature of God's love. Despite the younger son's mistakes and reckless behavior, the father welcomes him back without hesitation, demonstrating that God's love is always available to us, no matter how far we have strayed.

2. **The Joy of Reconciliation:** The celebration of the son's return signifies the joy and fulfillment found in reconciliation. God delights in our return to Him and rejoices when we come back to Him in repentance.
3. **Forgiveness and Acceptance:** The father's willingness to forgive and accept his son back into the family teaches us about the importance of forgiveness. It challenges us to extend grace and acceptance to others, just as we have received from God.

4. **The Danger of Resentment:** The elder brother's resentment reveals the danger of harboring feelings of entitlement and comparison. It highlights the need to recognize and appreciate the grace extended to others, rather than focusing on our own perceived sacrifices.

Reflections and Applications

To apply the wisdom of this parable in our lives, consider these reflections:

1. **Are there areas in your life where you need to embrace the unconditional love of God?** Reflect on any feelings of unworthiness or distance from God and allow His grace to fill those gaps.

2. **How can you celebrate and support those who have returned to faith or sought forgiveness?** Consider ways you can actively show love and acceptance to those who have made mistakes but are seeking reconciliation.

3. **Are you holding onto any resentment or comparisons?** Evaluate your own heart and work on letting go of bitterness or feelings of unfairness, focusing instead on the joy of others' returns to grace.

4. **How can you extend unconditional love and forgiveness in your relationships?** Identify practical steps you can take to offer grace and acceptance to others, reflecting the love of God in your interactions.

The Parable of the Prodigal Son reminds us of the transformative power of unconditional love and forgiveness. By embodying these principles, we can live in the fullness of God's grace and foster a spirit of compassion and joy in our own lives.

Chapter 3: The Lost Sheep

Introduction

The Parable of the Lost Sheep is a profound illustration of God's boundless love and the joy that comes from redemption. Found in Luke 15:3-7, this parable tells the story of a shepherd who leaves his ninety-nine sheep to search for one that has gone astray. Through this story, Jesus reveals deep truths about forgiveness, pursuit, and divine joy. The narrative encourages us to understand the value of every individual and the celebration that follows when what was lost is found.

Here is the full citation of the parable:

Luke 15:3-7 (NLT):

3. So Jesus told them this story:

4. "If a man has a hundred sheep and one of them gets lost, what will he do? Won't he leave the ninety-nine others in the wilderness and go to search for the one that is lost until he finds it?
5. And when he has found it, he will joyfully carry it home on his shoulders.

6. When he arrives, he will call together his friends and neighbors, saying, 'Rejoice with me because I have found my lost sheep.'

7. In the same way, there is more joy in heaven over one lost sinner who repents and returns to God than over ninety-nine others who are righteous and haven't strayed away!

Context and Meaning

To fully grasp the meaning of the Parable of the Lost Sheep, it's essential to understand the context in which Jesus told this story. The parable is part of a trilogy of parables found in Luke 15, which also includes the Parable of the Lost Coin and the Parable of the Prodigal Son. Each of these parables emphasizes different aspects of God's grace and the joy of reconciliation.

In the time of Jesus, shepherds were often seen as lowly and their work was considered menial. However, Jesus uses this common occupation to illustrate a profound spiritual truth. The shepherd in the story represents God, who is tirelessly committed to seeking out those who have wandered away from Him. The ninety-nine sheep symbolize those who are already in a safe place, while the one lost sheep represents each individual who is separated from God.

The parable begins with a shepherd who has a hundred sheep but loses one. Instead of being content with the ninety-nine, he leaves them in the open field and goes in search of the lost one. His search is diligent and passionate, and when he finally finds the lost sheep, he rejoices and calls his friends and neighbors to celebrate with him. Jesus concludes the parable by stating that there is more joy in heaven over one sinner who repents than over ninety-nine righteous people who do not need to repent.

Lessons of Search and Redemption

The Parable of the Lost Sheep teaches us several valuable lessons about search, redemption, and divine joy:

1. **The Value of the Individual:** Each person is precious in God's eyes, regardless of their circumstances or their past. The shepherd's willingness to leave the ninety-nine to find the one lost sheep highlights the immense value of each individual. This illustrates how God values every person and is willing to go to great lengths for their redemption.

2. **The Diligent Pursuit:** The shepherd's search for the lost sheep is persistent and earnest. This reflects God's relentless pursuit of those who are lost. It teaches us that no matter how far someone may have strayed, God's love and pursuit never waver.

3. **The Joy of Redemption:** The shepherd's joy upon finding the lost sheep signifies the joy in heaven when a sinner repents and returns to God. This celebration emphasizes the profound delight and gratitude that accompanies reconciliation and restoration.

4. **The Call to Compassion:** This parable encourages us to adopt a similar attitude of compassion and pursuit in our own lives. Just as the shepherd sought the lost sheep, we are called to reach out to those who are lost or in need, reflecting God's love and grace.

Reflections and Applications

To apply the wisdom of this parable in our daily lives, consider the following reflections:

1. **Reflect on Your Value:** Remember that you are valued and loved by God, no matter where you are or what you have done. Take comfort in knowing that God is always pursuing you with His love.
2. **Reach Out to the Lost:** Identify individuals around you who may be feeling lost or distant. Reflect on how you can reach out to them with compassion and support, demonstrating the love of God in practical ways.

3. **Celebrate Reconciliation:** When someone makes a positive change or returns to a path of faith, celebrate their journey and embrace the joy of redemption. Your support and encouragement can be a powerful testament to the grace of God.

4. **Embrace God's Pursuit:** Allow the truth of God's relentless pursuit to inspire you in your own spiritual journey. Understand that no matter how far you may wander, God is always ready to welcome you back with open arms.

The Parable of the Lost Sheep reminds us of the depth of God's love and the joy that comes from finding what was lost. By reflecting on these lessons, we can live in a way that mirrors God's grace and compassion, making a positive impact in the lives of those around us.

Chapter 4: The Lost Coin

Introduction

The parable of the Lost Coin is a beautiful illustration of God's deep and unwavering love for every individual. Found in Luke 15:8-10, this parable teaches us about the joy of restoration and the value of every single person in the eyes of God. Jesus tells this story to reveal the heart of divine grace and the lengths to which God goes to recover what is lost.

Through this parable, Jesus invites us to understand that just as a lost coin holds significant value to its owner, each person is precious to God. The story encourages us to appreciate the joy and celebration that come from finding and restoring what was once lost.

Context and Meaning

In the context of this parable, Jesus addresses the theme of lostness and recovery within the broader narrative of the lost sheep and the prodigal son. In Luke 15, Jesus uses three parables to illustrate how God rejoices over the return of those who are lost. The Lost Coin parable is particularly powerful as it underscores the meticulous and loving nature of God's pursuit.

The parable goes as follows:

Luke 15:8-10 (NLT):

8. "Or suppose a woman has ten silver coins and loses one. Won't she light a lamp and sweep the entire house and search carefully until she finds it?

9. And when she finds it, she will call in her friends and neighbors and say, 'Rejoice with me because I have found my lost coin.'

10. In the same way, there is joy in the presence of God's angels when even one sinner repents."

In this story, a woman who has ten silver coins loses one. The coin represents a significant part of her wealth, and she searches diligently until she finds it. Her joy upon finding the coin reflects the intense value and importance she places on it.

Lessons of Value and Restoration

The parable of the Lost Coin offers several key lessons about divine grace and the process of restoration:

1. **The Value of Each Individual:** Just as the lost coin is valuable to the woman, every person is precious to God. The story reminds us that no one is insignificant in God's eyes. Each person's return to God is celebrated with great joy.

2. **The Diligence in Seeking the Lost:** The woman's persistent search for the lost coin illustrates God's relentless pursuit of those who are lost. This teaches us that God does not give up on anyone, no matter how distant they may seem.

3. **The Joy of Restoration:** The joy and celebration the woman experiences when she finds the coin reflects the rejoicing in heaven when a lost person returns to God. This teaches us that restoration and reconciliation are causes for great celebration.

4. **The Importance of Community:** The woman shares her joy with friends and neighbors, demonstrating the communal aspect of rejoicing over restoration. This emphasizes the role of community in celebrating and supporting each other's journey back to God.

Reflections and Applications

To apply the wisdom of this parable to our daily lives, consider these reflections:

1. **Recognize Your Value:** Reflect on the idea that you are deeply valued by God. No matter how lost or distant you may feel, know that God sees you as precious and worth pursuing.
2. **Be Diligent in Seeking the Lost:** Just as the woman searched carefully for her coin, consider how you can be persistent in reaching out to those who are lost or in need of support. Your efforts can make a significant impact on their journey.

3. **Celebrate Restoration:** Embrace the joy that comes from witnessing restoration and reconciliation in your life and the lives of others. Celebrate these moments with gratitude and share the joy with your community.

4. **Support Each Other:** Be an active part of your community by celebrating and encouraging others in their spiritual journey. Offer support and rejoice together when someone returns to the faith or overcomes a challenge.

By understanding the value of each individual and the joy of restoration, we can live in alignment with the grace of God and actively participate in the process of bringing lost souls back to Him.

Chapter 5: The Sower

Introduction

The Parable of the Sower is a profound and insightful story that Jesus used to illustrate the different responses people have to the message of the Kingdom of God. Found in the Gospel of Matthew, chapter 13, verses 3-9, and also in Mark and Luke, this parable reveals important truths about spiritual receptivity and the growth of faith.

Jesus told this parable to convey how the Word of God is received by different kinds of people, using the imagery of a sower scattering seeds across various types of soil. Each type of soil represents a different response to God's message, and through this story, Jesus invites us to examine our own hearts and attitudes towards spiritual growth.

Context and Meaning

To fully understand the Parable of the Sower, it is essential to grasp its context and the imagery Jesus employed. In Jesus' time, farming was a common occupation, and sowing seeds was a familiar process. A sower would scatter seeds broadly, knowing that not all seeds would fall on fertile ground.

In the parable, Jesus describes a sower who goes out to sow seeds. Some of the seeds fall on the path and are quickly eaten by birds. Other seeds fall on rocky ground, where they sprout but wither due to a lack of roots. Some seeds fall among thorns, which choke the plants. Finally, some seeds fall on good soil and produce a bountiful harvest.

The key to understanding this parable lies in recognizing the different types of soil as representing different responses to the message of the Kingdom of God:

1. **The Path:** Represents those who hear the message but do not understand it. The devil quickly snatches away what was sown in their hearts.

2. **Rocky Ground:** Represents those who receive the message with joy but fall away quickly when faced with difficulties because their faith lacks deep roots.
3. **Among Thorns:** Represents those who hear the message, but the worries of life and the deceitfulness of wealth choke the Word, making it unfruitful.

4. **Good Soil:** Represents those who hear the message, understand it, and bear fruit with perseverance.

Here is the full citation of the parable from the New Living Translation (NLT):

Matthew 13:3-9 (NLT):

3. He told many stories in the form of parables, such as this one:"Listen! A farmer went out to plant some seeds.

4. As he scattered them across his field, some seeds fell on a footpath, and the birds came and ate them.

5. Other seeds fell on shallow soil with underlying rock. The seeds sprouted quickly because the soil was shallow.

6. But the plants soon wilted under the hot sun, and since they didn't have deep roots, they died.

7. Other seeds fell among thorns that grew up and choked out the tender plants.
8. Still other seeds fell on fertile soil, and they produced a crop that was thirty, sixty, and even a hundred times as much as had been planted!

9. Anyone with ears to hear should listen and understand."

Lessons on Receptivity and Spiritual Growth

The Parable of the Sower teaches several vital lessons about spiritual receptivity and growth:

1. **Understanding and Openness:** The parable emphasizes the importance of understanding and openness to the message of God. The condition of the soil represents how willing we are to receive and understand the message.

2. **Deep Roots and Perseverance:** The rocky soil illustrates the need for deep, rooted faith. Without a strong foundation, our spiritual growth is vulnerable to challenges and trials.

3. **Dealing with Distractions:** The seeds among thorns show how worldly concerns and distractions can hinder our spiritual growth. It is crucial to focus on God and avoid letting life's worries choke our faith.

4. **Fruitfulness:** The good soil represents a receptive heart that bears fruit. True spiritual growth results in a life that produces good works and reflects the love and grace of God.

Reflections and Applications

To apply the wisdom from the Parable of the Sower in our daily lives, consider these reflections:

1. **What is the condition of your heart?** Reflect on the type of soil that best represents your response to God's message. Are there areas where you need to cultivate a more receptive heart?

2. **How can you deepen your spiritual roots?** Identify practices that can help you build a stronger foundation in your faith, such as regular prayer, study of Scripture, and fellowship with other believers.

3. **What distractions or worries are choking your spiritual growth?** Take steps to address these concerns and focus on what truly matters in your relationship with God.

4. **Are you bearing fruit in your life?** Look for ways to live out your faith in practical ways, serving others and reflecting the love of God in your actions.

By embracing the lessons of this parable, we can grow spiritually and live lives that are fruitful and pleasing to God. May we all strive to be good soil, ready to receive and nurture the Word of God in our hearts.

Chapter 6: The Parable of the Mustard Seed

Introduction

The Parable of the Mustard Seed is a profound story told by Jesus to illustrate the nature of faith and the growth of God's kingdom. This parable, found in the Gospel of Matthew, chapter 13, verses 31-32, uses the imagery of a tiny mustard seed to reveal how something small can grow into something magnificent and impactful. Through this simple yet powerful metaphor, Jesus invites us to reflect on the power of faith and the expansive nature of God's work in our lives.

Jesus' parable serves as a source of encouragement and inspiration, reminding us that even the smallest acts of faith can lead to extraordinary outcomes. The story is not just about the growth of a seed but about the transformation that occurs when we place our trust in God.

Context and Meaning

To fully grasp the meaning of the Parable of the Mustard Seed, it's important to understand the context in which Jesus shared it. During Jesus' time, mustard seeds were known for their small size, yet mustard plants could grow to be quite large. This juxtaposition highlights the contrast between the seed's initial insignificance and its eventual significance.

In this parable, Jesus compares the kingdom of heaven to a mustard seed, which a man plants in his field. Although the seed is the smallest of all seeds, it grows into a tree that provides shelter for the birds of the air. This image serves as a metaphor for how the kingdom of heaven starts small—through the faith of individuals and the humble beginnings of Jesus' ministry—but grows into something vast and inclusive.

Here is the full text of the parable:

Matthew 13:31-32 (NLT):

31. Here is another illustration Jesus used: "The Kingdom of Heaven is like a mustard seed planted in a field.

32. It is the smallest of all seeds, but it becomes the largest of garden plants; it grows into a tree, and birds come and make nests in its branches."

This parable highlights the transformative power of faith. Just as the mustard seed grows into a large tree, so too does the kingdom of heaven expand from humble beginnings to encompass the entire world.

Lessons of Faith and Growth

The Parable of the Mustard Seed teaches several important lessons about faith and growth:

1. **The Power of Small Beginnings:** Jesus uses the mustard seed to show that even the smallest acts of faith can lead to significant results.

No matter how insignificant our efforts may seem, they have the potential to make a big difference in God's kingdom.

2. **The Transformative Nature of Faith:** Just as the mustard seed grows into a large tree, faith has the power to transform our lives and our surroundings. It starts small but, when nurtured, can produce profound change and growth.

3. **Inclusiveness and Expansion:** The growth of the mustard seed into a tree that shelters birds symbolizes the inclusive nature of God's kingdom. What begins as a small, personal faith can expand to embrace and bless many others.

Reflections and Applications

To apply the wisdom of this parable to our lives, consider the following reflections:

1. **How can we nurture and grow our faith, even if it seems small or insignificant?** Reflect on ways you can cultivate your faith through prayer, study, and action, understanding that even the smallest efforts can lead to significant spiritual growth.

2. **In what areas of your life can you see the impact of small beginnings leading to larger outcomes?** Consider examples from your own experiences where small acts of faith or kindness have led to greater results or blessings.

3. **How can we be more inclusive and supportive in our own communities, reflecting the expansive nature of God's kingdom?** Think about how you can reach out to others and provide support, mirroring the shelter and growth described in the parable.

Remember, the Parable of the Mustard Seed teaches us that great things often start from humble beginnings. By embracing and nurturing our faith, we participate in the growth and expansion of God's kingdom, contributing to a world that reflects His love and grace.

Chapter 7: The Parable of the Leaven

Introduction

The Parable of the Leaven, found in the Gospel of Matthew 13:33 and Luke 13:20-21, is a brief yet profound story that Jesus used to illustrate the nature of the Kingdom of Heaven. This parable, though simple in its imagery, carries deep implications about spiritual transformation and the growth of God's kingdom.

In this parable, Jesus compares the Kingdom of Heaven to yeast that a woman takes and hides in a large amount of flour until it works through the entire dough. This image of yeast, often overlooked, offers a powerful lesson about how God's influence gradually and profoundly changes the world and the lives of individuals.

Context and Meaning

To fully grasp the meaning of the Parable of the Leaven, it's essential to understand the context in which Jesus shared it. In the time of Jesus, leaven or yeast was a common household item used in baking. It works silently and invisibly, yet its effect on dough is undeniable and transformative.

Matthew 13:33 (NLT):

33. Jesus also used this illustration: "The Kingdom of Heaven is like the yeast a woman used in making bread. Even though she put only a little yeast in three measures of flour, it permeated every part of the dough."

Luke 13:20-21 (NLT):

20. He also asked, "What else is the Kingdom of God like?

21. It is like the yeast a woman used in making bread. Even though she put only a little yeast in three measures of flour, it permeated every part of the dough."

In these passages, Jesus uses the image of leaven to illustrate several key aspects of the Kingdom of Heaven:

1. **The Subtle Power of Transformation:** Just as a small amount of yeast can transform a large quantity of dough, the Kingdom of Heaven starts from small beginnings but has a powerful impact on

the world. Its influence might seem minor at first, but it gradually permeates and transforms everything it touches.

2. **The Invisible Work of God:** Yeast works invisibly within the dough, expanding and growing without being seen. Similarly, the work of God's kingdom often happens out of sight, gradually affecting people's lives and the world in profound ways.

3. **The Comprehensive Impact:** The leaven affects the entire dough, symbolizing how the Kingdom of Heaven influences all aspects of life. It spreads and grows until it reaches every part, showing that God's kingdom is all-encompassing and transformative.

Lessons of Transformation and Expansion

The Parable of the Leaven teaches us several important lessons about spiritual transformation and the growth of God's kingdom:

1. **Small Beginnings with Big Impact:** The parable reminds us that even small acts of faith and kindness can have a significant impact. The Kingdom of Heaven often starts in seemingly insignificant ways but grows to affect the entire world.

2. **Patience and Persistence:** Just as yeast takes time to leaven the dough, the work of God's kingdom often unfolds gradually. We are encouraged to be patient and persistent, trusting that God's work is progressing even if we cannot immediately see the results.

3. **Holistic Influence:** The leaven represents how the Kingdom of Heaven integrates into every part of our lives. It encourages us to allow God's influence to permeate all aspects of our being, from our personal lives to our interactions with others and our contributions to society.

4. **Transformation from Within:** The parable highlights that true transformation happens from within. Just as yeast changes the dough from inside, the Kingdom of Heaven transforms us internally, changing our attitudes, values, and behaviors.

Reflections and Applications

To apply the wisdom of the Parable of the Leaven in our daily lives, consider the following reflections:

1. **How can you allow small acts of faith to make a difference in your life and the lives of others?** Reflect on ways you can start with small, positive actions that align with the values of God's kingdom.

2. **In what areas of your life do you need to be patient and trust in the gradual work of transformation?** Identify areas where you may not see immediate results but need to remain hopeful and persistent.

3. **How can you ensure that the influence of God's kingdom affects every part of your life?** Consider how you can integrate spiritual principles into all aspects of your daily routine, relationships, and decisions.

4. **What internal changes is God prompting you to make?** Reflect on how God's influence is working within you, transforming your thoughts, attitudes, and actions to better align with His kingdom. The Parable of the Leaven invites us to recognize and embrace the subtle, yet powerful, work of God's kingdom. It encourages us to be patient and persistent, understanding that even the smallest beginnings can lead to significant, transformative outcomes.

Chapter 8: The Unjust Steward

Introduction

The Parable of the Unjust Steward is a thought-provoking story told by Jesus that is found in the Gospel of Luke, chapter 16, verses 1-13. This parable, sometimes known as the Parable of the Shrewd Manager, provides insight into the wise use of resources and the importance of being faithful in small things. It challenges us to consider how we manage our resources and relationships in the light of eternal principles.

Jesus shared this parable to teach His followers about the value of shrewdness and faithfulness. Although the steward in the story is initially portrayed as dishonest, Jesus uses his actions to illustrate deeper truths about stewardship and the proper use of wealth.

Context and Meaning

To grasp the full meaning of this parable, it's important to understand the context in which Jesus told it. The parable begins with a rich man who had a steward, or manager, who was accused of wasting the rich man's possessions. In response to this accusation, the rich man decides to fire the steward and demand an account of his management.

Facing imminent dismissal, the steward devises a plan to secure his future. He calls in each of his master's debtors and reduces their debts, hoping that they will show him favor once he is out of a job. Surprisingly, the master commends the dishonest steward for his shrewdness, highlighting that even though the steward acted dishonestly, he demonstrated wisdom in planning for his future.

Jesus concludes the parable with key lessons about the wise use of money and the importance of faithfulness. He underscores the idea that those who are faithful in small matters will also be trusted with larger responsibilities.

Here is the complete citation of the parable:

Luke 16:1-13 (NLT):

1. Jesus told this story to his disciples: "There was a certain rich man who had a manager handling his affairs. One day a report came that the manager was wasting his employer's money.

2. So the employer called him in and said, 'What's this I hear about you? Get your report in order, because you are going to be fired.'

3. "The manager thought to himself, 'Now what? My boss has fired me. I don't have the strength to dig ditches, and I'm too proud to beg.

4. Ah, I know how to ensure that I'll have plenty of friends who will give me a home when I am fired.'
5. "So he invited each person who owed money to his employer to come and discuss the situation. He asked the first one, 'How much do you owe him?'

6. The man replied, 'I owe him 800gallons of olive oil.' So the manager told him, 'Take the bill and quickly change it to 400gallons.'

7. "'And how much do you owe my employer?' he asked the next man. 'I owe him 1,000 bushels of wheat,' was the reply. 'Here,' the manager said, 'take the bill and change it to 800bushels.'

8. "The rich man had to admire the dishonest rascal for being so shrewd. And it is true that the children of this world are more shrewd in dealing with the world around them than are the children of the light.

9. Here's the lesson: Use your worldly resources to benefit others and make friends. Then, when your earthly possessions are gone, they will welcome you to an eternal home.

10. "If you are faithful in little things, you will be faithful in large ones. But if you are dishonest in little things, you won't be honest with greater responsibilities.

11. And if you are untrustworthy about worldly wealth, who will trust you with the true riches of heaven?

12. And if you are not faithful with other people's things, why should you be trusted with things of your own?

13. "No one can serve two masters. For you will hate one and love the other; you will be devoted to one and despise the other. You cannot serve both God and money."

The master's commendation of the steward's shrewdness is not an endorsement of dishonesty, but a recognition of the steward's cleverness in managing his situation. Jesus uses this story to teach His followers about the importance of being wise and responsible with the resources entrusted to us.

Lessons on Wisdom and Resource Management

The Parable of the Unjust Steward offers several valuable lessons on the use of resources and wisdom:

1. **Wise Use of Resources:** The steward's shrewdness highlights the importance of being wise and strategic in managing our resources. Although his actions were dishonest, his ability to plan for his future is commendable and serves as a lesson in the importance of foresight and prudent management.

2. **Faithfulness in Small Things:** Jesus emphasizes that faithfulness in small matters is crucial. Those who are reliable and trustworthy in handling small responsibilities will be entrusted with greater ones. This principle applies to all areas of life, including our financial management and personal integrity.

3. **Eternal Perspective:** Jesus teaches that our handling of material wealth should be done with an eternal perspective. By using our

resources wisely, we can build relationships and make a positive impact that extends beyond this life.

4. **Single-Minded Service:** The parable underscores the impossibility of serving both God and wealth. True discipleship requires a single-minded focus on God and His purposes, rather than being divided by the pursuit of material gain.

Reflections and Applications

To apply the wisdom from this parable in our lives, consider the following questions:

1. **How do we manage our resources?** Reflect on your current financial and material management. Are there ways you can be more strategic and prudent, even if it means making difficult decisions?

2. **Are we faithful in small responsibilities?** Evaluate your faithfulness in everyday tasks and responsibilities. How can you demonstrate reliability and trustworthiness in both small and large matters?

3. **Do we view our resources from an eternal perspective?** Consider how your use of resources aligns with eternal values. Are you using your wealth and possessions in ways that reflect your commitment to God's purposes?

4. **Are we serving God or material wealth?** Examine your priorities and allegiances. Are you allowing the pursuit of wealth to

overshadow your commitment to God? Seek to align your values and actions with divine principles.

By integrating these lessons into our daily lives, we can better manage the resources entrusted to us and reflect the wisdom and grace of God in our actions.

Chapter 9: The Parable of the Ten Virgins

Introduction

The Parable of the Ten Virgins is a compelling story told by Jesus to illustrate the importance of readiness and vigilance in our spiritual lives. Found in Matthew 25:1-13, this parable offers a profound lesson about being prepared for the coming of the Kingdom of Heaven. Jesus used this story to teach His followers about the need for spiritual preparedness and the consequences of neglecting to be watchful.

In this parable, Jesus contrasts the wise with the foolish, highlighting the difference between those who are prepared for His return and those who are not. By examining this parable, we gain insight into the nature of spiritual readiness and the importance of living with a sense of urgency and purpose.

Context and Meaning

To fully grasp the message of the Parable of the Ten Virgins, it is essential to understand the context in which Jesus told it. This parable is part of a series of teachings that Jesus gave about the end times, often referred to as the Olivet Discourse. In this discourse, Jesus used various parables to describe what the Kingdom of Heaven would be like and to prepare His followers for His eventual return.

In the story, ten virgins are waiting for the bridegroom to arrive. Five of them are wise and prepared, bringing extra oil for their lamps, while the other five are foolish and fail to bring sufficient oil. When the bridegroom arrives at midnight, the foolish virgins find that their lamps have gone out and are unable to join the wedding feast. They go to buy more oil, but by the time they return, the door is shut, and they are left out.

Here is the full citation of the parable:

Matthew 25:1-13 (NLT):

1. "Then the Kingdom of Heaven will be like ten bridesmaids who took their lamps and went to meet the bridegroom.

2. Five of them were foolish, and five were wise.

3. The five who were foolish didn't take enough olive oil for their lamps,

4. but the other five were wise enough to take along extra oil.

5. When the bridegroom was delayed, they all became drowsy and fell asleep.

6. "At midnight they were roused by the shout, 'Look, the bridegroom is coming! Come out and meet him!'

7. "All the bridesmaids got up and prepared their lamps.

8. Then the five foolish ones asked the others, 'Please give us some of your oil because our lamps are going out.'

9. "But the others replied, 'We don't have enough for all of us. Go to a shop and buy some for yourselves.'

10. "But while they were gone to buy oil, the bridegroom came. Then those who were ready went in with him to the marriage feast, and the door was locked.
11. Later, when the other five bridesmaids returned, they stood outside, calling, 'Lord! Lord! Open the door for us!'

12. "But he called back, 'Believe me, I don't know you!'

13. "So you, too, must keep watch! For you do not know the day or hour of my return.

The parable emphasizes the importance of being spiritually prepared and alert, as we do not know when the final reckoning will come. Jesus uses this story to illustrate that preparedness is crucial for entering into the joy of the Kingdom of Heaven.

Lessons on Preparation and Vigilance

The Parable of the Ten Virgins offers several key lessons about spiritual preparation and vigilance:

1. **Be Prepared:** The wise virgins' preparation with extra oil highlights the necessity of being spiritually ready at all times. This preparation involves cultivating a relationship with God, living according to His teachings, and being vigilant in our faith.

2. **The Importance of Vigilance:** The story underscores the need to remain watchful and alert. The foolish virgins' failure to prepare demonstrates that neglecting our spiritual responsibilities can lead to missed opportunities and exclusion from the Kingdom of Heaven.

3. **Individual Responsibility:** Each virgin was responsible for her own lamp and oil. This teaches us that spiritual readiness is a personal responsibility. We cannot rely on others to maintain our relationship with God; we must take ownership of our own spiritual journey.

4. **The Finality of Decisions:** The closing of the door symbolizes the finality of the decision regarding our preparedness. Once the opportunity is lost, it cannot be regained. This serves as a reminder to be diligent and not procrastinate in our spiritual commitments.

Reflections and Applications

To apply the wisdom of this parable to our lives, consider the following reflections:
1. **Am I Spiritually Prepared?** Reflect on your current state of spiritual readiness. Are you actively maintaining and nurturing your relationship with God, or are there areas where you need to be more diligent?

2. **How Can I Stay Vigilant?** Identify practical steps you can take to remain vigilant in your faith. This might include regular prayer, studying scripture, participating in worship, or engaging in acts of service.

3. **Do I Rely on Others for My Spiritual Growth?** Assess whether you depend on others for your spiritual development. Remember that personal responsibility is key; take charge of your own journey and seek to grow independently.

4. **What Are My Priorities?** Examine your priorities and how they align with your spiritual goals. Ensure that your actions and decisions reflect a commitment to being prepared for the coming of the Kingdom.

By reflecting on these questions and applying the lessons from the Parable of the Ten Virgins, you can live with a sense of purpose and readiness, ensuring that you are always prepared to enter into the joy of God's presence.

Chapter 10: The Rich Man and Lazarus

Introduction

The parable of the Rich Man and Lazarus is a profound story told by Jesus that appears in the Gospel of Luke, chapter 16, verses 19-31. This parable contrasts the lives of two men—one rich and one poor—and their destinies after death. It serves as a powerful reminder of the consequences of how we live our lives and how we treat others.

In this story, Jesus illustrates the concept of justice and mercy, challenging us to reflect on our attitudes towards wealth, poverty, and compassion. The parable provides a vivid picture of the eternal implications of our earthly actions and highlights the importance of heeding the wisdom of God's word.

Context and Meaning

To understand the parable fully, it's crucial to consider its context. Jesus told this parable to address the attitudes of the Pharisees, who were known for their love of money and their lack of empathy towards the poor. The rich man and Lazarus represent contrasting realities and the outcomes of their respective lives.

In the story, a rich man lives a life of luxury and indulgence, while a poor man named Lazarus suffers at his gate, covered in sores and longing for the scraps from the rich man's table. After death, Lazarus is carried to Abraham's side, a place of comfort, while the rich man finds himself in torment in Hades. The rich man, now in agony, begs

Abraham to send Lazarus to ease his suffering with a drop of water.
Abraham reminds him of the choices he made during his life and the
great chasm that now separates them, which cannot be crossed.

This parable highlights the reversal of fortunes in the afterlife and the
finality of the judgment that follows. It emphasizes that our actions
and attitudes towards others, especially the less fortunate, have
eternal significance.
Here is the full parable:

Luke 16:19-31 (NLT):

19. Jesus said, "There was a certain rich man who was splendidly
clothed in purple and fine linen and who lived each day in luxury.

20. At his gate lay a poor man named Lazarus who was covered with
sores.

21. As Lazarus lay there longing for scraps from the rich man's table,
the dogs would come and lick his open sores.

22. "Finally, the poor man died and was carried by the angels to be
with Abraham. The rich man also died and was buried,

23. and his soul went to the place of the dead. There, in torment, he
saw Abraham in the far distance with Lazarus at his side.

24. "The rich man shouted, 'Father Abraham, have some pity! Send
Lazarus over here to dip the tip of his finger in water and cool my
tongue. I am in anguish in these flames.'

25. *"But Abraham said to him, 'Son, remember that during your lifetime you had everything you wanted, and Lazarus had nothing. So now he is here being comforted, and you are in anguish.*

26. *And besides, there is a great chasm separating us. No one can cross over to you from here, and no one can cross over to us from there.'*

27. *"Then the rich man said, 'Please, Father Abraham, at least send him to my father's home.*

28. *For I have five brothers, and I want him to warn them so they don't end up in this place of torment.'*

29. *"But Abraham said, 'Moses and the prophets have warned them. Your brothers can read what they wrote.'*

30. *"The rich man replied, 'No, Father Abraham! But if someone is sent to them from the dead, then they will repent of their sins and turn to God.'*

31. *"But Abraham said, 'If they won't listen to Moses and the prophets, they won't be persuaded even if someone rises from the dead.'"*

Lessons of Justice and Mercy

The parable of the Rich Man and Lazarus teaches several critical lessons about justice and mercy:

1. **The Consequences of Ignoring the Needy:** The rich man's fate demonstrates the consequences of living a self-centered life without regard for the suffering of others. His indifference to Lazarus's plight

ultimately leads to his own suffering, underscoring the importance of compassion and generosity.

2. **The Reversal of Fortunes:** The parable illustrates a dramatic reversal in the afterlife, where Lazarus, who suffered on earth, is now comforted, while the rich man, who lived in luxury, faces torment. This reversal serves as a reminder of the ultimate justice of God and the eternal significance of our earthly actions.

3. **The Finality of Choices:** Abraham's response to the rich man's plea highlights the finality of judgment after death. The chasm between them signifies that the choices we make in this life have eternal consequences, and there is no opportunity for change once our earthly life is over.

4. **The Sufficiency of Scripture:** The rich man's request for a miraculous sign to convince his brothers is met with the assertion that the teachings of Moses and the prophets are sufficient. This teaches us that God has already provided everything we need to understand and follow His will through His Word.

Reflections and Applications

To apply the wisdom of this parable to our lives, consider the following reflections:

1. **Are We Aware of the Needs Around Us?** Reflect on how attentive you are to the needs of those who are less fortunate. Are

there ways you can be more compassionate and generous in your
daily life?

2. **How Do We Use Our Resources?** Evaluate how you use your
resources—time, money, and talents. Are they being used to help
others, or are they consumed by self-indulgence?

3. **What Is Our Attitude Towards Wealth?** Consider your attitude
towards wealth and possessions. Do you see them as blessings to be
shared or as something to be hoarded for personal comfort?

4. **Are We Responsive to God's Word?** Reflect on how you respond
to the teachings of Scripture. Are you attentive to the guidance
provided in the Bible, or do you seek additional signs and wonders?
The parable of the Rich Man and Lazarus challenges us to live with
awareness and compassion, understanding that our actions have
eternal consequences. By embracing the lessons of justice and mercy
taught by Jesus, we can align our lives with His wisdom and make a
meaningful difference in the world around us.

Chapter 11: The Hidden Treasure

Introduction

The parable of the Hidden Treasure is a profound illustration that
Jesus used to convey the unparalleled value of the Kingdom of
Heaven. Found in Matthew 13:44, this brief yet impactful parable
invites us to recognize the immeasurable worth of spiritual truths and
the transformative power of discovering them. In this story, Jesus uses

a simple yet striking image—a hidden treasure in a field—to reveal a deeper spiritual reality.

Context and Meaning

To fully appreciate the parable of the Hidden Treasure, it's important to understand its historical and cultural context. In Jesus' time, it was common for people to hide their valuables in fields or other secret places to protect them from theft or invasion. A field was often seen as a place where one might unexpectedly find something valuable.

In the parable, Jesus tells the story of a man who discovers a hidden treasure while working in a field. Recognizing its immense value, he hides it again and sells everything he owns to buy the field. The act of selling all his possessions to acquire the field demonstrates his deep understanding of the treasure's worth.

Here is the complete parable from the New Living Translation (NLT):

Matthew 13:44 (NLT):

44. *"The Kingdom of Heaven is like a treasure that a man discovered hidden in a field. In his excitement, he hid it again and sold everything he owned to get enough money to buy the field."*

The hidden treasure represents the Kingdom of Heaven—an extraordinary and invaluable gift from God. The man's willingness to sell all he has signifies the profound realization of its worth and the total commitment required to embrace it fully.

Lessons of Value and Spiritual Search

The parable of the Hidden Treasure imparts several key lessons about the value of spiritual discovery and the pursuit of divine truth:

1. **The Unmatched Value of the Kingdom:** The parable emphasizes that the Kingdom of Heaven is of such great value that it surpasses all worldly possessions and ambitions. It is a treasure worth everything one has, highlighting the need for us to recognize and prioritize spiritual wealth over material gains.

2. **Joy and Excitement in Discovery:** The man's reaction upon finding the treasure reflects the joy and excitement that comes with discovering spiritual truths. It reminds us that encountering and understanding God's Kingdom should bring immense joy and a sense of fulfillment.

3. **Total Commitment:** The man's decision to sell everything he owns to buy the field illustrates the total commitment required to fully embrace the Kingdom of Heaven. It is a call to evaluate our lives and be willing to make sacrifices for what is truly valuable.

4. **The Element of Discovery:** The fact that the treasure was hidden signifies that spiritual truths are often found through personal discovery and revelation. It encourages us to seek and explore the depths of God's Kingdom with diligence and an open heart.

Reflections and Applications

To apply the wisdom of the Hidden Treasure parable to our lives, consider the following reflections and questions:

1. **What is the value of the Kingdom of Heaven in your life?** Reflect on what the Kingdom of Heaven means to you personally and how it compares to your material possessions and pursuits.

2. **How do you respond to spiritual discovery?** Evaluate your excitement and joy when you uncover new truths about God's Kingdom and how that affects your spiritual journey.

3. **Are you willing to make sacrifices for spiritual growth?** Consider what you might need to give up or change in your life to fully embrace and live out the values of the Kingdom of Heaven.

4. **How can you seek and discover spiritual truths more effectively?** Explore practical ways to deepen your understanding of God's Kingdom, whether through prayer, study, or engagement with a faith community.

Remember, the parable of the Hidden Treasure challenges us to recognize the supreme value of spiritual truth and to be willing to invest wholeheartedly in our pursuit of the Kingdom of Heaven. By doing so, we align ourselves with the profound joy and fulfillment that come from living a life centered on divine values.

Chapter 12: The Pearl of Great Value

Introduction

The parable of the Pearl of Great Value, found in Matthew 13:45-46, is a profound illustration of the value of the Kingdom of Heaven. Jesus used this brief yet powerful story to teach us about the unparalleled worth of God's kingdom and the importance of prioritizing it above all else. This parable encourages us to examine our own lives and values, inviting us to recognize and embrace the ultimate treasure that is the Kingdom of Heaven.

In this chapter, we will delve into the meaning of the parable, uncover its lessons about sacrifice and priority, and explore practical ways to apply these teachings to our daily lives. By understanding the true value of the Kingdom, we are encouraged to live with purpose and devotion.

Context and Meaning

The parable of the Pearl of Great Value is part of a series of parables that Jesus used to describe the nature of the Kingdom of Heaven. Here is the complete passage from Matthew 13:45-46 in the New Translation Version (NLT):

Matthew 13:45-46 (NLT):

45. *"Again, the Kingdom of Heaven is like a merchant on the lookout for choice pearls.*

46. When he discovered a pearl of great value, he sold everything he owned and bought it!

In this parable, Jesus compares the Kingdom of Heaven to a merchant seeking fine pearls. When the merchant finds one pearl of extraordinary value, he sells everything he has to purchase it. This story illustrates the concept that the Kingdom of Heaven is worth more than anything else in life. The merchant's willingness to sell all his possessions to acquire the pearl emphasizes the supreme worth of the Kingdom.

The parable highlights the idea that recognizing the value of the Kingdom of Heaven requires a personal decision to prioritize it above all other concerns. It calls us to understand the transformative power of the Kingdom and to be willing to make sacrifices for its sake.

Lessons of Sacrifice and Priority

1. **The Supreme Value of the Kingdom:** Just as the merchant found a pearl of immense worth, so too does the Kingdom of Heaven hold a value beyond comparison. This teaches us to recognize the unparalleled worth of God's kingdom in our lives and to understand that it is a treasure that surpasses all earthly possessions and pursuits.

2. **Willingness to Sacrifice:** The merchant's decision to sell everything he owned to buy the pearl illustrates the importance of sacrifice. In the context of the Kingdom of Heaven, this means being willing to let go of anything that stands in the way of fully embracing and living out our faith. It encourages us to assess our priorities and

be ready to make sacrifices for the sake of our spiritual growth and commitment.

3. **Single-Minded Focus:** The merchant's focused pursuit of the pearl represents the need for a single-minded commitment to the Kingdom of Heaven. It calls us to align our values and actions with the teachings of Jesus, ensuring that our lives reflect our recognition of the Kingdom's supreme worth.

4. **Transformation and Value:** The parable teaches that discovering the true value of the Kingdom of Heaven can transform our lives. Just as the merchant's life was changed by acquiring the pearl, so too can our lives be transformed when we fully embrace and prioritize God's kingdom.

Reflections and Applications

To apply the wisdom of the Pearl of Great Value in our daily lives, consider the following reflections:

1. **What is the true value of the Kingdom of Heaven in your life?** Reflect on what the Kingdom means to you personally. How does its value influence your decisions and priorities?

2. **Are there things in your life that you need to let go of to fully embrace the Kingdom?** Identify any obstacles or distractions that may be hindering your spiritual growth. How can you address these to better align your life with the teachings of Jesus?

3. **How can you cultivate a single-minded focus on the Kingdom of Heaven?** Look for practical ways to ensure that your actions, thoughts, and values are consistently aligned with the principles of the Kingdom. This may involve setting specific goals, making intentional choices, and seeking guidance through prayer and study.

4. **In what ways has recognizing the value of the Kingdom transformed your life?** Consider how your understanding of the Kingdom has impacted your daily experiences, relationships, and overall perspective. How can you continue to grow in your appreciation of this divine treasure?

By embracing the lessons of this parable, we are encouraged to prioritize the Kingdom of Heaven above all else, making it the central focus of our lives. Through this commitment, we align ourselves with the wisdom and grace of God, finding true fulfillment and purpose.

Chapter 13: The Parable of the Talents

Introduction

The Parable of the Talents is a powerful story told by Jesus to teach about responsibility, stewardship, and the use of our God-given gifts. This parable, found in Matthew 25:14-30, illustrates the importance of making the most of the opportunities and resources entrusted to us.

Matthew 25:14-30 (NLT):

14. "Again, the Kingdom of Heaven can be illustrated by the story of a man going on a long trip. He called together his servants and entrusted his money to them while he was gone.

15. He gave five bags of silver to one, two bags of silver to another, and one bag of silver to the last—dividing it in proportion to their abilities. He then left on his trip.

16. "The servant who received the five bags of silver began to invest the money and earned five more.
17. The servant with two bags of silver also went to work and earned two more.

18. But the servant who received the one bag of silver dug a hole in the ground and hid the master's money.

19. "After a long time their master returned from his trip and called them to give an account of how they had used his money.

20. The servant to whom he had entrusted the five bags of silver came forward with five more and said, 'Master, you gave me five bags of silver to invest, and I have earned five more.'

21. "The master was full of praise. 'Well done, my good and faithful servant. You have been faithful in handling this small amount, so now I will give you many more responsibilities. Let's celebrate together!'

22. "The servant who had received the two bags of silver came forward and said, 'Master, you gave me two bags of silver to invest, and I have earned two more.'

23. *"The master said, 'Well done, my good and faithful servant. You have been faithful in handling this small amount, so now I will give you many more responsibilities. Let's celebrate together!'*

24. *"Then the servant with the one bag of silver came and said, 'Master, I knew you were a harsh man, harvesting crops you didn't plant and gathering crops you didn't cultivate.*
25. *I was afraid I would lose your money, so I hid it in the earth. Look, here is your money back.'*

26. *"But the master replied, 'You wicked and lazy servant! If you knew I harvested crops I didn't plant and gathered crops I didn't cultivate,*

27. *why didn't you deposit my money in the bank? At least I could have gotten some interest on it.'*

28. *"Then he ordered, 'Take the money from this servant, and give it to the one with the ten bags of silver.*

29. *To those who use well what they are given, even more will be given, and they will have an abundance. But from those who do nothing, even what little they have will be taken away.*

30. *Now throw this useless servant into outer darkness, where there will be weeping and gnashing of teeth.'*

In this parable, Jesus compares the kingdom of heaven to a master who entrusts his servants with various amounts of money (talents) before going on a journey. The story unfolds to reveal how each servant's actions reflect their understanding of their master's expectations and their commitment to fulfilling their responsibilities.

Context and Meaning

To fully grasp the meaning of this parable, it is important to understand the historical and cultural context in which Jesus told it. In Jesus' time, a "talent" was a substantial sum of money, often used as a unit of weight or currency. The parable uses this financial metaphor to convey deeper spiritual truths about how we handle the gifts and responsibilities given to us by God.

In the story, a master leaves on a journey and gives three of his servants different amounts of talents: five, two, and one. The first two servants invest their talents and double their amount, while the third servant buries his talent in the ground. Upon the master's return, he praises the first two servants for their faithfulness and rewards them with greater responsibilities. In contrast, the third servant is rebuked for his laziness and fear, and his talent is taken away.

This parable teaches us that our actions with the resources and opportunities we are given will be evaluated by God. It underscores the importance of being proactive and diligent in using our abilities for His purposes.

Lessons of Responsibility and Purpose

The Parable of the Talents provides several key lessons on responsibility and purpose:

1. **Stewardship of Gifts:** Each servant is entrusted with different amounts of talents, symbolizing that we all have different gifts and

resources. The parable teaches us that we are stewards of what we have been given and are expected to use our gifts responsibly.

2. **Accountability:** The master's return and the subsequent judgment highlight that we will be held accountable for how we use our resources and opportunities. God expects us to invest and utilize our talents effectively rather than burying them out of fear or complacency.

3. **Faithfulness and Reward:** The parable emphasizes that faithfulness in small things leads to greater responsibilities and rewards. The first two servants who used their talents wisely were rewarded with more, demonstrating that God values and rewards diligent and faithful stewardship.

4. **The Consequences of Inaction:** The third servant's decision to bury his talent illustrates the negative consequences of inaction and fear. The parable warns against failing to act and encourages us to overcome fear and take initiative in using our abilities.

Reflections and Applications

To apply the wisdom of the Parable of the Talents in our daily lives, consider the following reflections and questions:

1. **What Talents Have I Been Given?** Reflect on the unique gifts, skills, and resources you possess. How are you currently using them to make a positive impact?

2. **Am I Being a Faithful Steward?** Evaluate how you manage your talents and responsibilities. Are you using your gifts to their fullest potential, or are you holding back out of fear or uncertainty?

3. **How Can I Invest My Gifts for Greater Purpose?** Identify practical ways to use your abilities to serve others and contribute to God's work. Consider opportunities where you can be more proactive and take initiative.

4. **What Are the Consequences of My Choices?** Reflect on the potential outcomes of your decisions and actions. How might your choices affect your growth, impact, and relationship with God?

Remember that the Parable of the Talents calls us to be diligent and proactive in using our gifts. By embracing our responsibilities and investing our talents wisely, we honor God and fulfill our purpose in His kingdom.

Chapter 14: The Parable of the Two Sons

Introduction

The Parable of the Two Sons is a profound story told by Jesus to illustrate the difference between outward obedience and genuine repentance. Found in Matthew 21:28-32, this parable highlights the importance of aligning our actions with our words and the transformative power of true repentance.

In this parable, Jesus contrasts two sons who are asked by their father to work in his vineyard. Their responses and subsequent actions reveal a deeper truth about obedience and the condition of the heart. Through this story, Jesus invites us to reflect on our own responses to God's call and the sincerity of our repentance.

Context and Meaning

The parable is set in the context of Jesus' teachings in Jerusalem, where He is addressing religious leaders and challenging their understanding of righteousness. The vineyard represents God's work and His call to live according to His will. The two sons symbolize different responses to God's call.

1. **The First Son:** Initially refuses to work in the vineyard but later repents and goes.
2. **The Second Son:** Promises to work but does not follow through with his promise.

By contrasting these two responses, Jesus illustrates that true obedience involves more than just words; it requires action and a genuine change of heart. The parable criticizes those who appear righteous but fail to act on their promises, and it commends those who, despite initial reluctance, eventually align their actions with God's will.

Here is the full passage from the New Living Translation (NLT):

Matthew 21:28-32 (NLT):

28. "But what do you think about this? A man with two sons told the older boy, 'Son, go out and work in the vineyard today.'

29. The son answered, 'No, I won't go.' But later he changed his mind and went anyway.

30. Then the father told the younger son, 'You go.' And he said, 'Yes, sir, I will.' But he didn't go.

31. "Which of the two obeyed his father?" they replied, "The first." Then Jesus explained his meaning: "I tell you the truth, corrupt tax collectors and prostitutes will get into the Kingdom of God before you do.

32. For John the Baptist came and showed you the right way to live, but you didn't believe him, while tax collectors and prostitutes did. And even when you saw this happening, you refused to believe him and repent of your sins."

In this passage, Jesus uses the actions of the two sons to challenge the religious leaders, who, despite their outward appearances of righteousness, have failed to recognize and embrace the message of repentance and change brought by John the Baptist.

Lessons of Obedience and Repentance

The Parable of the Two Sons teaches several important lessons about obedience and repentance:

1. **The Importance of Genuine Obedience:** True obedience to God goes beyond mere promises. It is demonstrated through actions that

align with our words. The first son's eventual obedience shows that repentance and change of heart are more significant than initial resistance.

2. **The Power of Repentance:** Repentance is a vital aspect of our relationship with God. It involves recognizing our mistakes, changing our minds, and taking action to align ourselves with God's will. The first son's change of heart exemplifies the transformative power of true repentance.

3. **The Rejection of Hypocrisy:** Jesus criticizes those who claim righteousness but fail to act on it. The parable challenges us to examine our own lives for any discrepancies between our professed beliefs and our actual behavior.

4. **Inclusiveness of God's Grace:** The parable illustrates that God's grace extends to those who are often marginalized or considered sinners. Even those who have initially resisted can receive grace if they truly repent and follow God's ways.

Reflections and Applications

To apply the wisdom of this parable to our lives, consider the following reflections:

1. **How do our actions align with our promises?** Reflect on areas in your life where there may be a gap between what you say and what you do. Strive to close that gap by ensuring that your actions reflect your true intentions.

2. **Are we willing to repent and change when we recognize our mistakes?** Embrace the opportunity to repent and make amends, just as the first son did. This openness to change is crucial in maintaining a genuine relationship with God.

3. **How can we avoid hypocrisy in our faith?** Examine your life for any inconsistencies between your professed beliefs and your daily actions. Commit to living out your faith authentically and with integrity.

4. **Do we extend grace to others as God extends grace to us?** Consider how you can show grace and understanding to those who may not initially appear righteous but are seeking change. This reflects the inclusive nature of God's love.

Remember, the essence of this parable lies in living out our faith with authenticity and humility. By aligning our actions with our words and embracing true repentance, we demonstrate the genuine heart that God desires.

Chapter 15: The Wicked Tenants

Introduction

The Parable of the Wicked Tenants is a profound story told by Jesus to illustrate the consequences of rejecting God's messengers and the divine Son. Found in the Gospel of Matthew, Chapter 21, verses 33-46, this parable not only addresses the immediate audience but also speaks to the enduring principles of justice, accountability, and divine grace.

In this story, Jesus uses the metaphor of a vineyard—a symbol of God's kingdom—to convey His message. The vineyard represents God's care and provision, while the wicked tenants symbolize those who fail to honor and respect God's authority. Through this parable, Jesus reveals the consequences of ignoring God's commands and the inevitability of justice.

Parable Citation:

Matthew 21:33-46 (NLT):

33. *"Now listen to another story. A certain landowner planted a vineyard, built a wall around it, dug a pit for pressing out the grape juice, and built a lookout tower. Then he leased the vineyard to tenant farmers and moved to another country.*

34. *At the time of the grape harvest, he sent his servants to collect his share of the crop.*

35. *But the farmers grabbed his servants, beat one, killed one, and stoned another.*

36. *So the landowner sent a larger group of his servants to collect for him, but the results were the same.*

37. *"Finally, the owner sent his son, thinking, 'Surely they will respect my son.'*

38. "But when the tenant farmers saw his son coming, they said to one another, 'Here comes the heir to this estate. Come on, let's kill him and get the estate for ourselves!'

39. So they grabbed him, dragged him out of the vineyard, and murdered him.

40. "When the owner of the vineyard returns," Jesus asked, "what do you think he will do to those farmers?"
41. The religious leaders replied, "He will put the wicked men to a horrible death and lease the vineyard to others who will give him his share of the crop after each harvest."

42. Then Jesus asked them, "Didn't you ever read this in the Scriptures? 'The stone that the builders rejected has now become the cornerstone. This is the lord's doing, and it is wonderful to see.'

43. I tell you, the Kingdom of God will be taken away from you and given to a nation that will produce the proper fruit.

44. Anyone who stumbles over that stone will be broken to pieces, and it will crush anyone it falls on."

45. When the leading priests and Pharisees heard this parable, they realized he was telling the story against them—they were the wicked farmers.

46. They wanted to arrest him, but they were afraid of the crowds, who considered Jesus to be a prophet.

Context and Meaning

To fully appreciate the Parable of the Wicked Tenants, it's essential to understand the context in which Jesus told it. At this time, Jesus was in Jerusalem, and His teachings were challenging the religious leaders and their understanding of God's kingdom. The vineyard metaphor would have resonated strongly with the Jewish audience, as vineyards were commonly used in Scripture to represent Israel.

In the story, a landowner establishes a vineyard and leases it to tenant farmers. When harvest time arrives, he sends his servants to collect the fruit, but they are mistreated and killed. Eventually, he sends his son, whom the tenants also kill, hoping to claim the vineyard for themselves.

Jesus uses this story to illustrate the rejection of God's prophets and, ultimately, His Son, Jesus. The landowner's actions symbolize God's patience and justice, while the tenants' actions represent the failure of the religious leaders to recognize and respect divine authority.

The message of this parable is clear: God's patience has limits, and rejecting His messengers and Son will lead to divine retribution. However, it also emphasizes that God's kingdom will be given to those who produce the right fruits of righteousness and justice.

Lessons of Divine Justice and Grace

The Parable of the Wicked Tenants offers several key lessons about divine justice and grace:

1. **Accountability to God:** The parable highlights that all people are accountable to God. The vineyard represents God's blessings and responsibilities entrusted to humanity. Failure to respect and honor God's commands results in consequences.

2. **Rejection of God's Messengers:** Just as the tenants mistreated and killed the landowner's servants, people often reject and oppose God's messengers. This rejection is a serious offense that leads to judgment.

3. **The Importance of Fruitfulness:** Jesus emphasizes that the kingdom of God is given to those who produce good fruit. This fruit symbolizes righteous actions and living in accordance with God's will.

4. **The Role of Jesus as the Cornerstone:** The parable concludes with a reference to Psalm 118:22, where Jesus identifies Himself as the cornerstone. The rejection of this cornerstone results in spiritual brokenness, while acceptance leads to the foundation of a new and fruitful life.

Reflections and Applications

To apply the wisdom of this parable to our daily lives, consider the following reflections:

1. **How do we respond to God's messengers?** Reflect on how you receive and act upon God's guidance through various means, whether it's through scripture, teachings, or personal convictions.

2. **Are we producing the right fruit in our lives?** Examine your life for evidence of righteousness and justice. Are you living in a way that reflects God's kingdom values?

3. **How do we honor Jesus as the cornerstone of our faith?** Recognize Jesus' central role in your life and faith. Build your life upon His teachings and example.

Remember that this parable serves as both a warning and an invitation. It warns against rejecting God's authority and the consequences of such actions, while also inviting us to embrace the grace and opportunities offered through Jesus.

By understanding and applying these lessons, we can live in a way that honors God's kingdom and fulfills the divine purpose for our lives.

Conclusion

As we reach the end of this journey through the parables of Jesus, let us pause to reflect on the profound wisdom and divine grace embedded within His teachings. The parables are not mere stories; they are timeless truths that call us to a higher understanding of God's kingdom and our place within it.

Through these parables, Jesus offers us a glimpse into the heart of God—His boundless love, mercy, and justice. We have learned about the Good Samaritan's selfless compassion, the Prodigal Son's redemptive forgiveness, the persistent widow's unwavering faith, and the humble tax collector's repentant heart. Each story invites us to see ourselves in the characters, to understand our flaws and our potential for transformation through God's grace.

The Parable of the Wicked Tenants, with which we conclude this book, serves as a sobering reminder of the consequences of rejecting God's messengers and His Son. Yet, it also underscores the unrelenting patience and love of our Creator, who continually reaches out to us, offering opportunities for repentance and renewal. The cornerstone that the builders rejected has become the foundation of our faith—Jesus Christ, the source of our salvation and the ultimate expression of God's love.

As we go forth from these reflections, let us carry the lessons of these parables in our hearts. Let us strive to live lives that bear good fruit, marked by love, compassion, humility, and faithfulness. Let us be ever mindful of our accountability to God, recognizing that we are stewards of His blessings and ambassadors of His kingdom.

May these parables inspire us to deeper faith and greater commitment to living out the principles of God's kingdom. Let us be the light in the darkness, the salt of the earth, and the hands and feet of Christ in a world that so desperately needs His love and truth.

In the end, the wisdom of Jesus' parables is not just for understanding but for living. As we apply these divine truths to our lives, we will experience the fullness of God's grace and the joy of His presence. Let us go forth with hearts transformed and spirits renewed, ready to serve and glorify God in all that we do.

Credits

"The Wisdom of Jesus: Parables That Transform Lives"
by Albert Barzaga

Author Note: Albert Barzaga is a pen name for Ramón Alberto Bárzaga Sánchez.

Acknowledgments: I am profoundly grateful to God for the wisdom and guidance that inspired and enabled me to create and design this book. Your divine support has been a source of strength and creativity throughout this journey.

Thank you for reading this book. For more updates and content, follow me on Pinterest: https://www.pinterest.com/pastoralbertbarzaga